AR PTS: 3.0

WORLD IN
FOCUS

FOCUS ON
CHINA

ALI BROWNLIE BOJANG AND NICOLA BARBER

WORLD ALMANAC® LIBRARY

Please visit our web site at: www.worldalmanaclibrary.com
For a free color catalog describing World Almanac® Library's list of high-quality books
and multimedia programs, call 1-800-848-2928 (USA) or 1-800-387-3178 (Canada).
World Almanac® Library's fax: (414) 332-3567.

Library of Congress Cataloging-in-Publication Data

Brownlie Bojang, Ali, 1949-
     Focus on China / by Ali Brownlie Bojang and Nicola Barber.
        p. cm. — (World in Focus)
     Includes bibliographical references and index.
     ISBN 0-8368-6216-3 (lib. bdg.)
     ISBN 0-8368-6235-X (softcover)
     1. China—Textbooks. I. Barber, Nicola. II. Title. III. World in Focus
(Milwaukee, Wis.)
     DS706.B75   2006
     951—dc22   2005054070

This North American edition first published in 2006 by
World Almanac® Library
A Member of the WRC Media Family of Companies
330 West Olive Street, Suite 100
Milwaukee, WI 53212 USA

Commissioning editor: Victoria Brooker
Editor: Nicola Barber
Inside design: Chris Halls, www.mindseyedesign.co.uk
Cover design: Hodder Wayland
Series concept and project management by EASI-Educational Resourcing (info@easi-er.co.uk)
Statistical research: Anna Bowden

World Almanac® Library editor: Alan Wachtel
World Almanac® Library cover design: Scott Krall

Population Density Map © 2003 UT-Battelle, LLC. All rights reserved.
Data for population density maps reproduced under licence from UT-Battelle, LLC.
All rights reserved.
Maps and graphs: Martin Darlison, Encompass Graphics

Picture acknowledgements:
The author and publisher would like to thank the following for allowing their pictures to be
reproduced in this publication:
Corbis 9 (top) (Burstein Collection), 9 (bottom), 14 and 54 (Keren Su), 11 and 13 (Bettmann),
15, 16, 17, 23, 24 and 26 (Reuters), 18 (Kin Cheung/Reuters), 21 (Andrew Holbrooke), 22
(Guang Nin/Reuters), 27 and 40 (China Photos/Reuters), 29 (China Span, LLC), 30 and 31
(Claro Cortes IV/Reuters), 36 (Corbis), 45 (top) (Bohemian Nomad Picturemakers), 45 (bottom)
(China Newsphoto/Reuters), 49 (Jason Lee/Reuters), 51 (Issei Kato/Reuters), 55 (Craig Lovell),
58 (Yang Liu), 59 (Wang Jianmin/Xinhua Photos); EASI-Images title page, 12, 19, 28, 33, 34, 38,
39, 41, 53 and 56 (Adrian Cooper), 4, 32, 47 and 48 (Tony Binns), 37 (Roy Maconachie); Chris
Fairclough cover, 5, 8, 10, 20, 25, 42, 43, 50 and 52; Ed Parker 57.

The directional arrow portrayed on the map on page 7 provides only an approximation of north.
The data used to produce the graphics and data panels in this title were the latest available at the
time of production.

CONTENTS

1 China – An Overview   4

2 History   8

3 Landscape and Climate   14

4 Population and Settlements   18

5 Government and Politics   22

6 Energy and Resources   26

7 Economy and Income   30

8 Global Connections   34

9 Transportation and Communications   38

10 Education and Health   42

11 Culture and Religion   46

12 Leisure and Tourism   50

13 Environment and Conservation   54

14 Future Challenges   58

Time Line   60

Glossary   61

Further Information   62

Index   63

Cover: Great Wall, north of Beijing.

Title page: Great Wall, Simatai.

CHAPTER 1

China – An Overview

China covers a vast area of eastern Asia and is home to one-fifth of the world's total population. Its culture and history stretch back nearly four thousand years, making it one of the oldest civilizations in the world. The Chinese once believed that their country was at the center of the geographical world, and they named it *Zhongguo*, meaning "Middle Earth" or "Middle Country." The name *China* probably comes from one of the early dynasties that ruled the country, the Qin (Ch'in).

▼ These spectacular limestone hills are found in the valley of the Li River, near Guilin, in Guanxi Province, south China. Fields of rice cover the floor of the valley.

▲ East and West meet on Nanjing Road, in Shanghai, a wide shopping street where people can buy anything from live scorpions to Ford cars. People can also buy food twenty-four hours a day from traditional street vendors or Western fast-food outlets.

RAPID CHANGE

Today, no other country in the world is changing as fast, and as dramatically, as China. For thousands of years, however, China changed very little. It was ruled by a series of dynasties, and the vast majority of the population worked the land. In the early twentieth century, China threw off its dynastic rule, and in 1949, it became a Communist state. Toward the end of the century, China's government introduced huge reforms that led to the country becoming one of the major world economies. Some international organizations now predict that China will overtake the United States and Europe to become the world's largest economy in about 2007.

While the vast majority of Chinese people have yet to benefit from China's economic boom, and millions still live in poverty, for some the changes have meant more affluence and an increasingly Western lifestyle. The factors that made China's economic growth possible— abundant natural resources, a large workforce, good infrastructure, and a stable society—have long been there. In the past, however, China was reluctant to develop relationships with other countries. Today, China's wealth is based on manufacturing and exporting products to the rest of the world. This change has involved a major shift in the thinking of the Communist party, which still governs China.

BIG POPULATION, BIG COUNTRY

China has the largest population of any country. In 2005, its population was estimated to be 1.3 billion. The size of its population is one of China's strengths, giving it a large workforce and a massive internal consumer market. At the same time, the Chinese government is faced with the challenge of feeding and ensuring the welfare of this vast populace.

Geographically, China is the third-largest country in the world, after Russia and Canada, and it has a huge range of different landscapes and climates. In the past, its vast size hindered its development, but today many new railways and roads are being built, and there has been a massive increase in air traffic within the country to move people and goods around quickly and efficiently. These changes, and

many others, make China a country that is a fascinating mix of the ancient and the ultra-modern, the traditional and the high-tech.

Physical Geography Data

- Land area: 3,600,927 square miles/ 9,326,400 square kilometers
- Water area: 104,459 sq miles/ 270,550 sq km
- Total area: 3,705,386 sq miles/ 9,596,950 sq km
- World rank (by area): 3
- Land boundaries: 13,753 miles/22,130 km
- Border countries: Afghanistan, Bhutan, Burma, India, Kazakhstan, North Korea, Kyrgystan, Laos, Mongolia, Nepal, Pakistan, Russia, Tajikistan, Vietnam
- Coastline: 9,005 miles/14,500 km
- Highest point: Mount Everest (29,035 feet/ 8,850 meters)
- Lowest point: Turpan Pendi (-505 ft/-154 m)

Source: CIA World Factbook

► The red color of China's flag symbolizes revolution. The large star represents the Communist party while the four smaller stars signify the four main social classes: peasants, workers, bourgeoisie, and capitalists. The flag was adopted in 1949.

RUSSIAN FEDERATION

KAZAKHSTAN

MONGOLIA

KYRGYZSTAN

JUNGGAR PENDI

Urumqi

TIEN SHAN

TARIM BASIN

TAKLA MAKAN DESERT

KUNLUN SHAN

ALTUN SHAN

QILIAN SHAN

QAIDAM PENDI

Qinghai Hu

Xining

Lanzhou

PLATEAU OF TIBET

HIMALAYAS

NEPAL

Mount Everest 29,035 ft

BHUTAN

BANGLADESH

INDIA

Lhasa

Brahmaputra

Salween

Mekong

C H I N A

Chengdu

SICHUAN PENDI

Chongqing

Yangtze River

Guiyang

Kunming

Xi River

Nanning

MYANMAR (BURMA)

Bay of Bengal

THAILAND

LAOS

VIETNAM

CAMBODIA

Gulf of Tongking

Haikou

GOBI

INNER MONGOLIA

Huhot

Baotou

Datong

Yinchuan

Taiyuan

Xianyang

Xi'an

Luoyang

Handan

Shijiazhuang

Jinan

Zhengzhou

Xuzhou

Xinyang

Nanjing

Hefei

Wuhan

Hangzhou

Nanchang

Changsha

Fuzhou

Shantou

Guangzhou

Kowloon

Macao

Xianggangdao (Hong Kong)

MANCHURIAN PLAIN

Qiqihar

Harbin

Jilin

Changchun

Fushun

Shenyang

Anshan

Tangshan

BEIJING

Tianjin

Dalian

N. KOREA

S. KOREA

Qingdao

Yellow Sea

Yellow River

Shanghai

East China Sea

TAIWAN

South China Sea

PHILIPPINES

Amur

Legend

★ Capital
● Cities > 5,000,000
● Cities > 2,500,000
• Cities > 1,000,000
▲ Mountain

0   200   400   600 kilometers
0   200   400   600 miles

N

120° 130° 50°

90° 30°

40° 80° 110° 100° 130°

30° 30°

80°

90° 100° 110° 20° 20° 120°

CHAPTER 2

History

For most of its four-thousand-year history, dynasties of emperors ruled China. One of the earliest dynasties, the Chou (771–481 B.C.), introduced the first feudal system—well over one thousand years before such a system existed in Europe. Under the feudal system, supporters of the emperor were given domains, or areas of land, in return for their loyalty, as well as for military and other services. The land of these domains was worked by peasants, who produced food and wealth for their lords and received protection in return.

ANCIENT CHINA

Over the centuries, China's borders expanded and contracted following conquests and incursions. Most dynasties were eventually brought down by revolutions, rebellions, or invasions. The times between dynasties were often periods of chaos during which various warlords vied for power. The threat of invasion from Central Asia led to the construction of the Great Wall of China. The wall was built during the Qin dynasty, beginning in about 214 B.C., to prevent incursions by Mongol tribes. It was extended westward during the Han dynasty. Over the centuries, it was rebuilt and extended several times more.

◀ Tourists from all over the world, including many from China itself, flock to see the Great Wall, which is located north of Beijing. The wall extends about 4,000 miles (6,400 kilometers) across northern China.

CHINESE DYNASTIES

Date	Dynasty
c.2000–c.1500 B.C.	**Xia** Some of the world's first towns built.
c.1700–c.1027 B.C.	**Shang** Writing system developed.
771–481 B.C.	**Chou** Feudal system established.
453–221 B.C.	Warring States period.
221–206 B.C.	**Qin** First unification of China as a centralized state; military expeditions push forward the frontiers in the north and south; construction of the Great Wall begins to deter invaders from Central Asia.
206 B.C.–A.D 220	**Han** Flourishing of intellectual, literary, and artistic life; paper and porcelain invented; improved methods for planting crops; westward expansion; trade with Central Asia starts along the "Silk Road."
A.D. 220–588	**Wei, Shu,** and **Wu** Period of chaos and decline; China divided into three kingdoms; growth of Taoism and Buddhism.
581–618	**Sui** Reunification and centralization of government.
618–907	**T'ang** High point in Chinese civilization; golden age of literature and art.
907–960	Several dynasties struggle for power; China experiences military invasions and breaks up into separate states.
960–1279	**Sung** Reunification of China; development of cities as centers of trade and industry;
1215	Mongols, led by Genghis Khan, capture Beijing.
1279–1368	**Yuan** Kublai Khan (grandson of Genghis Khan) captures the rest of China and establishes Yuan dynasty; Mongols begin to lose their power in the fourteenth century.
1368–1644	**Ming** Mongols driven out of Beijing; population doubles and economy booms.
1644–1911	**Ch'ing** or **Manchu** Expansion of territory; in the late nineteenth century, foreign governments gain control over parts of China.

◀ This bronze vessel dates back to the early Shang dynasty.

Focus on: Confucius

The philosophies of Confucius (K'ung Fu-tzu; c.551-c.479 B.C.) have had a great influence on the Chinese national character. Confucius emphasized the importance of the social order. From this basic idea, he developed an elaborate set of rules by which he thought people ought to live. He taught his ideas to over three thousand disciples who recorded his teachings in a book called the *Analects*. Confucius's ideas about the importance of learning and family and social ties were used as the basis of law from the Han dynasty (206 B.C.–A.D. 220) onward. His ideas also spread to other countries such as Japan, Korea, and Vietnam.

▶ This bronze statue of Confucius stands outside the Confucius Temple in Nanjing, in eastern China.

CHINA AND EUROPE

For centuries, China outpaced the rest of the world in the arts and sciences. During the T'ang dynasty (618–907), the capital city, Ch'ang-an (today known as Xi'an), was the largest city anywhere in the world, with a population of over one million people. (London and Paris did not reach this size for another one thousand years.) Chinese inventions such as the compass, the abacus, fireworks, and gunpowder impressed Western visitors to China. One of the first Europeans to go to China was the Venetian Marco Polo. Marco Polo left Venice in 1271 and spent more than fifteen years in China before returning home in 1295 with stories of the country's efficient postal system, the use of coal as a fuel, and a canal-based transport system.

European interest in trading with China started as early as the sixteenth century, but the Chinese emperors had little interest in the goods offered by the European traders. The emperors were suspicious of foreigners, fearing that they would attempt to gain power in China, and of the Christian missionaries who tried to establish their faith in China. In 1760, the Chinese government restricted European merchants to the southern port of Guangzhou.

THE OPIUM WARS

By the beginning of the nineteenth century, China was exporting huge amounts of products such as tea and silk to Europe. But while many European countries and the United States were increasingly interested in opportunities for trade with China, the Chinese emperor stated that China had "no need" for foreign products. One import, however, was becoming increasingly popular in China—opium. The opium trade was seen by the British government as one solution to its trade imbalance with China, and during the eighteenth century, British merchants brought increasing quantities of the drug into China. The increased availability of

▼ The Hall of Supreme Harmony, located in the Imperial Palace, in Beijing, was built in the fifteenth century. It was used for ceremonial occasions.

◀ The British navy bombards Guangzhou in 1841, during the First Opium War.

opium had a devastating effect on Chinese society, as thousands of people became addicted to it. In 1800, China banned opium. Britain and China fought the First Opium War (1839–1842) after China seized illegal stocks of opium in Guangzhou. China lost and, under the Treaty of Nanjing, the country opened several ports to foreign trade and ceded the island of Hong Kong to the British. After defeat in the Second Opium War (1858–1860) and a disastrous war against Japan (1894–1895), China was forced to cede more territory, allow more foreign access to its ports, and trade.

THE END OF THE DYNASTIES

By the beginning of the twentieth century, foreign demands and internal rebellions had completely eroded the power of the Ch'ing dynasty. In 1911, revolutionary forces led by Sun Yat-Sen finally deposed the last Ch'ing emperor, ending three thousand years of dynastic rule in China. China was proclaimed a republic in 1912. The revolutionary forces joined together to create the Nationalist party (Kuomintang). Almost immediately, however, rival warlords began fighting for power. At the end of World War I, under the terms of the Treaty of Versailles, China again lost territory when Japan was allowed to take over former German territories in China. On May 4, 1919, a group of students demonstrated against the treaty in Tiananmen Square in Beijing. This demonstration was part of a wave of nationalism that became known as the Fourth of May movement and which led to the formation of the Chinese Communist party in 1921. During the 1920s, the Communists and the Nationalists—led by Chiang Kai-shek after the death of Sun Yat-Sen in 1925—tried to work together to reunify China.

Focus on: The Boxer Uprising

The Boxers was a secret society whose members wanted to throw all the "foreign devils" (foreigners) out of China. In 1900, thousands of young people attacked symbols of European power and influence, such as embassies and Christian missions. They marched to Beijing, attracting more followers on the way, and laid siege to areas of the city for two months. Eventually, an international force of European and American soldiers put down the rebellion.

▲ This huge portrait of Mao Zedong hangs at Tiananmen Gate, the main entrance to the Imperial Palace in Beijing.

NATIONALISTS AND COMMUNISTS

The alliance between the Nationalists and the Communists quickly became strained. In 1927, Chiang Kai-shek's Nationalists attacked the Communists and forced many Communist leaders to go into hiding. The Nationalists established a government with its capital at Nanjing, and beginning in 1931, fought a civil war against the Communists. In the same year, however, Japan occupied Manchuria and advanced across northern China. Full-scale war between Japan and China broke out in 1937. Both the Nationalists and the Communists fought a guerrilla campaign against the Japanese invaders, but after the surrender of Japan in 1945, at the end of World War II, civil war between the two sides resumed.

During the war with Japan, the Communists had become both strong and popular under their leader, Mao Zedong, and it was the Communists who emerged victorious in the years after World War II. By 1949, they had defeated the Nationalists, forcing Chiang Kai-shek and his supporters to flee to Taiwan, an island off the east coast of China. There, with U.S. support, the Nationalists set up an alternative Chinese government. In Beijing, Mao Zedong proclaimed the creation of the world's second Communist state (after the Soviet Union), the People's Republic of China.

THE GREAT LEAP FORWARD

With help from its ally, the Soviet Union, Communist China made economic progress in the 1950s. Rapid industrialization increased production, and land was redistributed to create

Focus on: The Long March (1934–1935)

After the alliance between the Nationalists and the Communists came to an end in 1927, the Nationalists, who were better led and better equipped, inflicted heavy defeats on the Communists. In 1934, after several years of fighting, about one hundred thousand people—the main force of the Communist army—left their base in Jiangxi Province and marched west and then north for over 6,000 miles (9,650 km) in a journey that became known as the Long March. The twenty thousand Communist survivors joined other Communists in Yan'an a year later. In spite of the heavy losses during the Long March, Mao Zedong was able to take control of the Communist army and turn it into the force that eventually defeated the Nationalists.

agricultural cooperatives. In 1958, however, Mao Zedong introduced a policy—called the "Great Leap Forward"—that is estimated to have cost the lives of up to thirty million people.

The aim of the Great Leap Forward was to increase food and steel production through the creation of larger collective farms and new steel mills. Mao Zedong thought the Communist Party could inspire the Chinese people to work ever harder and overcome all obstacles. In reality, the Great Leap Forward was badly planned and led. By 1961, after a countrywide famine, the government was forced to admit its costly failure. Mao stepped down from power and was replaced by Liu Shaoqi, a modernizer who was more open to liberal approaches.

THE CULTURAL REVOLUTION

Mao Zedong soon became unhappy about what he saw as the "capitalist tendencies" of Liu Shaoqi and his supporters. Gradually, Mao regained influence, and in 1966, he launched the Great Proletarian Cultural Revolution. In the name of education and restoring true Communist principles, Mao's followers attacked intellectuals and those who they saw as bringing "bourgeois influences" into China. Students and workers denounced reformers and intellectuals in mass meetings. The Red Guards, a group made up mostly of school and university students, increasingly used violence against anyone they considered "bourgeois" or "elitist." Millions were forced into labor (or "reeducation," as it was called), many thousands were executed, temples and churches were destroyed, and schools were shut down. In 1968, Mao disbanded the Red Guards and the army restored order, leaving Mao and a small group of his supporters, sometimes called the Gang of Four, in power.

THE BEGINNINGS OF ECONOMIC REFORM

Mao Zedong died in 1976. Following his death, there was a struggle between those in the Communist party who believed China should open up to the rest of the world and develop economically (the "reformers"), and those who opposed such measures (the "conservatives"). The reformers, led by Deng Xiaoping, gained the upper hand, and in 1978, a period of economic modernization began. Trade was opened up to the outside world, and farmers were allowed to sell their surplus crops on the open market. Relations with Western countries also improved. U.S. president Richard Nixon visited China in 1972, establishing the first links that resulted in the restoring of full diplomatic relations between the United States and China in 1979. The current Chinese premier, Wen Jiabao, is seen as one of a long line of reformers who welcomes economic ties with the United States and other Western countries.

▼ Red Guards paraded through the streets of Beijing in 1967, during the Cultural Revolution. They carried flags and a portrait of Mao Zedong.

CHAPTER 3

Landscape and Climate

China covers an area of 3,705,386 sq miles (9,596,960 sq km). It is slightly larger than the United States and almost forty times the size of Britain. As someone might expect of such a vast country, China's landscapes include almost every type of terrain found anywhere on Earth—mountains, deserts, forests, and plains. Two-thirds of the country is uplands and mountains, much of which is inhospitable. Less than one-third of China's land is suitable for farming. The Yangtze River serves as a dividing line between the northern and southern regions of the country.

▼ Two bactrian camels in the Takla Makan Desert, which lies in Xinjiang Province, in far northwestern China.

THE NORTH AND WEST

The north and west are dominated by some of the most mountainous areas in the world, with heights averaging 14,764 feet (4,500 m) above sea level. The world's highest mountain range, the Himalayas, lies partly within China. The Himalaya region is remote, barren, and unsettled and forms a natural barrier between China and its western neighbors. To the north of the Himalayas lies a vast area of deserts and high pastures, including the Tibetan plateau.

THE SOUTH AND EAST

From the high altitudes of the west, the land descends toward the low-lying river plains in the east. Many rivers flow into this area, fed by

▲ Floodwaters from the Yangtze River inundate houses in Wuhan, the capital of Hubei Province, on August 27, 2002. The Yangtze floods every year, but the floods are worse in some years than in others.

melting snow and ice from the mountains, and the alluvial soils that they deposit create extremely fertile floodplains. This area has been farmed for centuries, and it is where the majority of China's population lives today.

CHINA'S RIVERS

The Chang Jiang, or Yangtze River, and the Huang He, or Yellow River, are China's most important rivers and support millions of people. They can, however, bring great destruction when they flood. The Huang He is known as "China's Sorrow" because of its regular and destructive floods. In the 1930s, an estimated five million people were drowned when the Huang He burst its banks on two separate occasions.

Focus on: The "Roof of the World"

Covering an area of around 965,000 sq miles (2.5 million sq km)—about one-quarter of China's land area—the Tibetan plateau dominates western China. About 80 percent of this highland plateau lies above 9,850 feet (3,000 m), and about half of it is over 14,764 feet (4,500 m). In the far west of the country, the Tibetan plateau meets the Himalayas. Fourteen of the world's peaks over 26,250 feet (8,000 m) lie within the Chinese border. The highest peak in the world, Mount Everest, which reaches an altitude of 29,035 feet (8,850 m), is on the border between China and Nepal. It is little wonder that the Tibetan plateau is known as "the roof of the world."

CHINA'S CLIMATES

Due to its vast size and its varied terrains, China has many different climates, which have seasons ranging from bitter, subarctic northern winters to warm, subtropical southern summers. Its climate is dominated by the great seasonal wind reversal known as the Asiatic monsoon. From May to September, warm, moist air is drawn into China from the Indian and Pacific Oceans, bringing rain. From October to April cool, dry air blows out from the center of Asia. China's climate is also influenced by altitude.

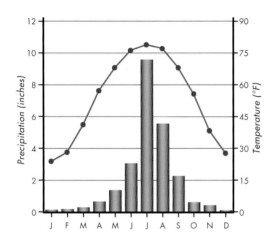

▲ Average monthly climate conditions in Beijing

? Did You Know?

Despite its huge size, China uses only one time zone—Greenwich Mean Time (GMT) plus eight hours. Because China covers a longitude range of about sixty degrees, the country lies across five international time zones, from plus five to plus nine hours GMT. China's use of only one time zone means that the country's far northwest doesn't get dark until after midnight.

▼ Police patrol the snow-covered rooftops of Beijing's Imperial Palace in December 1999. Winters in China's capital city can be bitterly cold.

THE NORTH AND WEST

Temperatures are extreme in China's northern and western areas. They are affected by the high altitude and, in winter, by the cold, dry air that blows from Siberia, which lies to the north. During the long winters, temperatures can sometimes fall as low as -27 °Fahrenheit (-33 °Celsius) in northern Manchuria—so cold that rivers freeze. Sand dunes covered in snow make an unusual sight in the desert areas. In contrast, daytime temperatures in the summer can reach 117 °F (47 °C) in the desert regions of the northwest and 100 °F (38 °C) in Beijing. Dust storms blow up in the deserts in April and May, often carrying sand to cover northern cities such as Beijing. In July and August, rainfall is high in Beijing, and the climate becomes humid and uncomfortable. In the country's far north and west, however, rainfall is more unpredictable, and in some desert areas, there is no rainfall.

TIBET

Tibet is one of the harshest places on Earth. The thin, high-altitude air can neither radiate nor absorb heat, creating extreme temperatures during the day and at night. In the summer, temperatures can reach up to 84 °F (29 °C) during the day and fall to below 32 °F (0 °C) at night. During the winter, average minimum temperatures of 14 °F (-10 °C) feel much colder because of the winds, which create wind chill.

THE SOUTH AND EAST

Southern and eastern China are partly within the tropics. In the summer, it is the warmest and wettest part of China, as moist air masses from the Pacific Ocean move inland. Summers are generally hot and humid, with average daytime temperatures around 86 °F (30 °C). Monsoon rainfall is high in the summer, and typhoons are a possibility along the southeast coast between July and September. On average, about five typhoons a year hit the region. Winter temperatures average 64 °F (18 °C), with regular rainfall.

▼ A man walks through the rubble of collapsed buildings after a typhoon hit Shanghai in July 2002. Five people died during the storm.

CHAPTER 4

Population and Settlements

With a huge population of nearly 1.3 billion people, China is the most populous nation on Earth. China's population has grown rapidly since the founding of the People's Republic, doubling in size between 1949 and 1987.

ETHNIC GROUPS

There are fifty-six different ethnic groups in China. The Han Chinese make up 92 percent of the population, overwhelmingly dominating China. China also has fifty-five officially recognized ethnic minorities. The largest minority group, the Zhuang, mostly live in Guangxi Province, an autonomous region in the south. The Hui, who are a group of Chinese Muslims, are the second largest ethnic minority. They live mainly across the north and central areas of the country. Other minorities include Uyghurs, who live in Xinjiang Province in the northwest; Tibetans; the Hakka people; and the Mongols, who are descended from the nomadic tribes to the north of China.

▼ The Hakka have a tradition of constructing circular buildings made from earth, such as these buildings in Xiayang, Fujian Province, in eastern China. About thirty thousand of these structures, which were originally built as a defense against bandits and invaders, exist.

THE ONE-CHILD POLICY

In the 1970s, the Chinese government realized that the country's rapid population growth was harmful to social and economic development, because it became increasingly difficult and costly to ensure employment, housing, and medical care for everyone. In 1979, the government began to implement a policy called the One-Child Policy to control population growth. In accordance with this policy, every birth has to be approved by family-planning officials, and couples face huge fines if they have more than one child. Second children cannot be registered, so they do not qualify for education or health-care support.

The restrictions of the One-Child Policy have since been relaxed for some people. Couples from ethnic minorities, parents who are themselves single children, and parents whose first child has been born with physical or mental disabilities may all apply for permission to have second children. Couples in rural areas may also be permitted to have another child if their first baby is a girl.

As a way to control population growth, the policy has been successful: birth rates have steadily declined. In 1969, the birth rate was 34.11 per thousand people; by 1998, it had dropped to 16.03 per thousand. The five-year plan for 2001-2005 aims to lower the annual population growth rate below 9 per thousand. The policy, however, has had other, far-reaching effects. It has created a population that is rapidly aging, resulting in fewer people to support the elderly. In addition, Chinese parents generally prefer to have sons, particularly in rural areas where many people want a child capable of coping with the physical demands of farming.

Despite government attempts to encourage people to value female babies, the practices of aborting female babies and of abandoning unwanted girls in orphanages have been widespread since the One-Child Policy was put into effect. One result is an imbalance in the Chinese population, with men outnumbering women by almost twelve to one, especially in rural areas. The One-Child Policy has also led to second children being concealed from the authorities. It is possible that there are tens of millions of unregistered children in China.

▲ This poster in a village in the province of Guizhou, in southeastern China, promotes the Chinese government's One-Child Policy.

? Did You Know?

The One-Child Policy has resulted in a generation of single, male children who are often referred to as China's "little emperors" because they are so spoiled.

POPULATION DENSITY

Although China's population growth has slowed dramatically, the number of people in China is still increasing by over nine million every year because of its large population base. Experts predict that China's population may reach nearly 1.5 billion by 2050, although China is likely to be surpassed by India in about 2035 as the world's most populous country.

The population is unevenly spread throughout the country. The average population density in China is 354.4 people per sq mile (136.8 per sq km). In the river valleys of the east, population density is more than 1,036 people per sq mile (400 per sq km), and in the central areas, there are 518 people per sq mile (200 per sq km). In the vast, sparsely populated plateaus of the west, however, there are fewer than 26 people per sq mile (10 per square km).

▼ Construction workers labor on a building project in the city of Xi'an, in central China.

URBANIZATION

Most people in China live in rural areas and farm the land. But as the country's economy develops, increasing numbers of people are being attracted to the towns and cities to find work and to escape poverty. Many of these

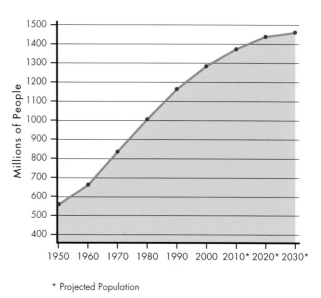

* Projected Population

▲ Population growth, 1950–2030

workers travel from place to place, working on big engineering and building projects before moving to find work elsewhere. Thousands of women have moved from the rural areas of Sichuan to work in electronics factories in the province of Guangdong, in the southeast.

In 1950, only 12 percent of China's population lived in urban areas; by 2001, the figure was 39 percent. China now has thirty-three cities in which the population exceeds one million, and by 2015, the majority of China's population is expected to be urban. Rapid urbanization and a big migratory workforce present the government with major problems. Cities are generally overcrowded, with families living in one or two rooms that are often rented from the company for which they work. China is expecting its urbanization rate to grow by 1 percent every year, as increasing numbers of rural residents turn to nonagricultural work to earn more and boost their standards of living.

Population Data

- Population: 1.3 billion
- Population 0–14 yrs: 24%
- Population 15–64 yrs: 69%
- Population 65+ yrs: 7%
- Population growth rate: 0.7%
- Population density: 354.4 per sq mile/ 136.8 per sq km
- Urban population: 39%
- Major cities: Beijing 10,849,000
                Shanghai 12,665,000
                Tianjin 9,346,000

Source: United Nations and World Bank

Focus on: Shanghai

Shanghai started as a busy fishing village at the mouth of the Yangtze River. It was one of the first Chinese ports opened up to foreign trade in the nineteenth century. Today, it has become China's biggest city. It has a registered population of 12.7 million, but it is estimated that at least three million unregistered migrant workers live in the city. Although the city has a negative birth rate, the number of people moving to it from rural areas is set to increase the city's population rapidly. One proposal for housing Shanghai's growing population is the construction of a three-hundred-story skyscraper that would reach 3,700 feet (1,128 m) high and house one hundred thousand people. If it was built, it would be the world's tallest building.

▶ New apartment buildings in Shanghai's Pudong district tower over the ramshackle houses in which many people live.

CHAPTER 5

Government and Politics

Since 1949, the Communist party has ruled China. The basic goal of the Chinese Communist state is to provide the "iron rice bowl"—welfare for all, from the cradle to the grave. For decades, China's government tried to provide the iron rice bowl using a totalitarian system.

▲ The Chinese National People's Congress—China's parliament—opens at the Great Hall of the People in Beijing in March 2004.

THE WORK UNIT

The Communist government still has representatives in the army, universities, and workplaces. Beginning in the 1950s, every Chinese adult was a member of a *danwei*— a work unit. Each danwei was managed by a member of the Communist party, who had great power over the day-to-day lives of its members, including involvement in their housing, health care, education, and freedom to travel away from home. With the introduction of economic reforms after 1978, however, the role of the danwei has become much weaker, particularly as employment has become increasingly flexible.

HUMAN RIGHTS ISSUES

The Chinese government places severe restrictions on freedom of speech, the media, religion, and workers' rights. Dissidents who speak out against the Communist government are often imprisoned or forced to live in exile. Many dissidents have been put in prison for petitioning for government reform, organizing workers, worshipping outside state-controlled venues, or using the Internet to call for government reform.

In 1989, a massive student demonstration for democratic reform began in Tiananmen Square in Beijing. People from all walks of life joined the students. When the protesters demanded that the country's leadership resign, the government answered by sending in troops to repress the demonstration. It is estimated that up to twenty-six hundred civilians were killed in this crackdown.

POLITICAL CHANGE

China's economic boom has resulted in huge differences in wealth between different parts of the country. Some of the southern provinces, which have benefited most from economic reform, have challenged the authority of the central Communist government in Beijing. Other countries have seized on this opportunity to put pressure on China to uphold human rights and to consider some degree of democratization as a way of holding together this vast country in the future.

Focus on: Repression of Religion

Since 1949, the Chinese government has suppressed all forms of religion. Falun Gong is a spiritual movement based on Buddhist practices. It started in China in the early 1990s and quickly acquired millions of followers. The government, however, was nervous about the threat to its authority posed by Falun Gong, and it banned the movement in 1999. Many Falun Gong leaders have been arrested and imprisoned. Similarly, Tibetan Buddhist monks and nuns who refuse to denounce their religious leader, the Dalai Lama, have been arrested and imprisoned or expelled from China.

▼ Falun Gong followers demonstrate against the Chinese government in Hong Kong in April 2001. Although Falun Gong is banned in mainland China, it remains legal in Hong Kong.

INTERNAL STRUGGLES

Throughout its history, China has gained and lost land. Originally, it covered the region around the Huang He (Yellow River). Since that time, it has expanded in all directions and was at its largest during the T'ang (618–907), Yuan (1279–1368), and Ch'ing (1644–1911) dynasties. As a result of various wars and disputes, some geographical areas in China remain in conflict today.

▼ The exiled Tibetan leader, the Dalai Lama, greets his followers during a visit to a Buddhist monastery in Calcutta, India, in September 2001.

TIBET

Tibet is a region of central Asia and the home of the Tibetan people. Chinese troops invaded Tibet in 1950, forcing the Tibetan government, led by the Dalai Lama, to go into exile in northern India. While the Tibetan government still claims sovereignty over Tibet, China claims that Tibet has always been part of its territory. In 1965, Tibet became an autonomous region of China called Xizang Zizhiqu. (*Zizhiqu* means "autonomous region" in Chinese.) Since 1989, the Chinese government has supported the systematic settlement of Han Chinese in Tibet. So many Han Chinese have been moved to Tibet that they threaten to outnumber the indigenous Tibetans, further diminishing any chances of Tibet gaining independence.

SPECIAL ADMINISTRATIVE REGIONS

At the end of the First Opium War, Britain forced China to give up the island of Hong Kong. More territories came under British control under later treaties, but in 1997, the whole colony reverted to China. In 1984, Britain and China came to a compromise agreement that resulted in Hong Kong becoming a Special Administrative Region (SAR) of China. Under this agreement, China promised that it would not impose its Communist economic system on Hong Kong, and that Hong Kong would retain its independence in all matters apart from defense and foreign affairs. This agreement

▲ Hong Kong's harbor at night, seen from the steep slopes of Victoria Peak on Hong Kong Island. Hong Kong has maintained its economic success since becoming one of China's special administrative regions in 1997.

will last until 2034. Until then, Hong Kong has its own elected government, separate membership in international organizations, and its own currency, the Hong Kong dollar.

China's other SAR is Macao, which is also on its south coast. Macao became a Portuguese colony in 1887. It was handed back to China in 1999 under an agreement similar to the one made about Hong Kong, which guaranteed "one country, two systems" for fifty years.

TAIWAN

In 1683, the island of Taiwan became part of the Ch'ing Empire. Officially, this island off China's southeast coast is still part of China, but it broke away from mainland control in 1949

when the defeated Nationalist government fled to there. While Taiwan has its own democratically elected government and is independent of China, the government of mainland China still claims that Taiwan is under its rule and refuses to have diplomatic relations with any country that recognizes Taiwan as a separate nation. Although the United States withdrew formal recognition from Taiwan in 1979, when it recognized the People's Republic of China, the United States still adopts the "two-China" approach, ensuring Taiwan's security while insisting that there will be no military action by Taiwan against China. Taiwan has thrived as a free market economy and, along with Hong Kong, has given China a model of how it may develop economically in the future.

CHAPTER 6

Energy and Resources

China has abundant natural resources, including massive energy resources and large reserves of minerals, timber, and water. According to figures released in 2003 by the Chinese government, China has reserves of 158 different minerals and is third in the world in terms of its total quantity of mineral reserves.

ENERGY SOURCES

China is the world's biggest producer and consumer of coal. Chinese coal accounts for one-third of all the coal mined in the world, and coal provides 61 percent of China's total energy requirements. China also has substantial reserves of oil, estimated by a Chinese oil expert at 16.75 billion tons (15.2 billion metric tons), or about 12 percent of the world's total reserves. China's domestic consumption of oil, however, is projected to reach 336 million tons (305 metric tons) by 2010, by which time China will have to import half of its oil supplies. There are vast untapped reserves of oil and natural gas in the Tarim Basin, an area the size of France in the province of Xinjiang, in the far western part of the country. Gas production in this region started in 2005, and the gas is pumped through a west-east pipeline, 2,610 miles (4,200 km) to the east of the country.

One important alternative to using fossil fuels such as coal, oil, and gas as a source of energy is hydroelectric power (HEP). Many of China's rivers flow through steep-sided valleys, providing the ideal conditions for building

▼ Rescuers help a worker out of a coal mine at Benxi, in the northeastern province of Liaoning, after the mine flooded in March 2002.

dams and harnessing the power of the water for HEP. Although HEP is a much more environmentally friendly source of energy than coal or oil, it has its drawbacks. The controversial Three Gorges Dam project on the Yangtze River has included the construction of the world's largest dam, 1.2 miles (2 km) in length and 607 feet (185 m) high. The reservoir behind the dam will cover 244 sq miles (632 sq

▼ Water gushes through the open sluice gates of the massive Three Gorges Dam on the Yangtze River.

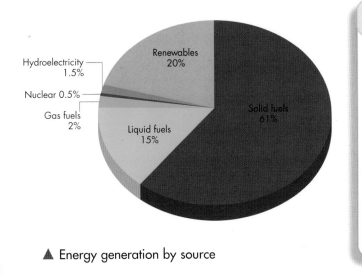

Hydroelectricity 1.5%

Nuclear 0.5%

Gas fuels 2%

Renewables 20%

Liquid fuels 15%

Solid fuels 61%

▲ Energy generation by source

Energy Data

🗁 Energy consumption as % of world total: 11.3

🗁 Energy consumption by sector (% of total):
   Industry: 49
   Transportation: 9
   Agriculture: 4
   Services: 2
   Residential: 36

🗁 CO_2 emissions as % of world total: 13.2

🗁 CO_2 emissions per capita in tons per year: 2.75

Source: World Resources Institute

km), but its creation has flooded a vast area of agricultural land and submerged the homes of two million people, forcing them to move. The project was started in 1993. It is due to be completed in 2009, when its twenty-six generators will be able to generate one-ninth of China's total electricity.

ENERGY CONSUMPTION

Demand for energy is rising rapidly in China and is exceeding supply. China's energy use in 2003 was about double its energy use in 1980. In contrast, energy use in the United States was slightly less in 2003 than in 1980. China's energy consumption is projected to keep growing dramatically.

In 2003, China was the world's second largest consumer (after the United States) of petroleum products. Its consumption of oil is now larger than its production, so China imports oil from the Middle East and Russia. Coal is also vitally important in China's economic development.

Between 1971 and 1996, the demand for coal increased five times over, with alarming consequences for the environment as a result of the increase in mining. By 2004, however, improved energy efficiency, environmental regulations, and new energy sources had slowed down the use of coal a little. Nuclear plants have also been developed as a "cleaner" way of producing energy.

WATER RESOURCES

China has two of the world's longest rivers, the Yangtze and the Huang He. Water is crucial to China's industries, farms, and homes. Although China is the fifth richest nation in water resources (after Brazil, Russia, Canada, and the United States), its reserves are very unevenly distributed. While there are ample water supplies south of the Yangtze River, parts of China north of the Yangtze have severe water

▼ A villager washes vegetables at a communal tap in Shiqing, Guizhou Province, in southeastern China.

shortages. The South-to-North Water Transfer Project aims to address this problem.

MINERAL RESOURCES

China has a wide range of important mineral resources. Most of China's minerals are found in the northeastern and central parts of the country. They include titanium, a rare and valuable metal used in joint-replacement surgery, and tungsten, which is used in the manufacture of light bulbs. China is also a major producer of tin, antimony, zinc, molybdenum, lead, and mercury, as well as ferrous metals such as iron, manganese, and vanadium.

FISHING

China is the world's largest fishing nation, with a catch of around 47.4 million tons (43 million metric tons) per year. Fish such as hairtail, chub mackerel, and black scraper are found in the vast coastal fisheries in the Bohai, Yellow, East China, and South China Seas. Inland freshwater fisheries are also important for catches of species such as carp, trout, and salmon.

▲ This fisherman is using two cormorants to catch fish, a traditional method of fishing. The picture was taken in 2000 on the Li River in Guangxi Province.

? Did You Know?

Of the world's forty-five thousand dams over 50 feet (17 m) in height, more than twenty-two thousand are in China.

Focus on: The South-to-North Water Transfer Project

In December 2002, China began a gigantic south-to-north water diversion project that is expected to take fifty years to complete and cost U.S. $59 billion. The main aim of the project is to alleviate the water shortages in northern China, particularly around Beijing and Tianjin and in the province of Hubei, by diverting water from southern China. The project involves building three canals to carry water to the drought-ridden areas. The canals will cross the eastern, middle, and western parts of China, linking the country's four major rivers—the Yangtze, the Huang He, the Huaihe, and the Haihe. Critics of this massive project are concerned about how it may damage the environment in the area from which the water originates. They argue that the solution to China's water problems lies not in moving water but in measures such as water conservation and improved irrigation efficiency.

CHAPTER 7

Economy and Income

After the death of Mao Zedong, and the victory of the reformers, China began to modernize its economy. Since 1978, China has gone from being a centrally controlled economy dominated by state-owned industry to an economy in which the market is determined by the supply and demand of goods.

THE OPEN-DOOR POLICY

It was Deng Xiaoping who started the transformation of China's economy. Before 1978, China's main trading partners were the Soviet Union and other Communist states, and its economy was centrally planned and tightly controlled by the Communist government. In the years after 1978, China encouraged foreign investment in order to provide the money to build new businesses and to bring in new technology—the so-called Open-Door Policy. In 1980, direct foreign investment in China totaled U.S.$6.25 billion. By 2002, this figure had risen to U.S.$448 billion.

Most of China's economic growth has been focused in the southern part of the country. Since 1980, five special economic zones (SEZs) have been set up along the south coast. Zhuhai, Shenzhen, and Shantou are in the province of Guangdong. Xiamen is in Fujian. The island province of Hainan is also an SEZ. The SEZs were created to encourage foreign businesses to invest in China through preferential tax policies and other incentives, as well as to be centers of science and industry. In 1984, the Communist

Economic Data

- Gross National Income (GNI) in U.S.$: 1,417,301,000,000
- World rank by GNI: 6
- GNI per capita in U.S.$: 1,100
- World rank by GNI per capita: 133
- Economic growth: 9%

Source: World Bank

◄ Chinese workers assemble DVD players for export to the United States and Europe at a factory in Zhenjiang, Jiangxi Province, in eastern China.

government also created a coastal zone of cities, reaching from Dalian in the north to Zhanjiang and Beihai in the south, where foreign investment was encouraged. This "open" zone has since been extended, with particular success in the Pudong New Zone in Shanghai, which has attracted many foreign-funded banks and businesses. Since 1992, China's government has also opened up some cities near its land borders, as well as the capitals of autonomous regions.

EXTERNAL AND INTERNAL MARKETS

In the five years up to 2002, Chinese exports increased by more than 50 percent, to U.S.$325 billion. Since then, they have been accelerating at 20 percent every year. China mainly exports to the United States (21 percent), Hong Kong (17 percent), Japan (13.6 percent), South Korea (4.6 percent), and Germany (4 percent), although the huge range of goods that it produces are found all over the world. Many of these products are high-tech electronic goods, such as DVD players, cellular phones, and flat-screen monitors, but China is also a major exporter of clothing and textiles, toys and sporting goods, minerals, and foodstuffs.

In the boom areas of the south and east, some Chinese people have themselves become important new consumers with vastly increased spending-power. Cellular phones and cars are particularly popular consumer items in China. It is estimated that one out of every three people in China will own a cellular phone in 2005. Although the proportion of the

▼ Chinese consumers inspect new cars at the "All in Auto 2004" exhibition in Shanghai. For those people in China who can afford them, large, expensive cars are important status symbols.

? Did You Know?

The world's largest shoe factory is in Guangdong. It employs eighty thousand people.

"new rich" is very small, China's population is so vast that even if only 1 percent of people can afford a car, that small percentage is a market of thirteen million people. Today, car ownership in China is rising dramatically, with the country's automobile sector growing by about 22 percent a year at a time when the automobile industry in Europe and the United States is growing by only 2 percent a year.

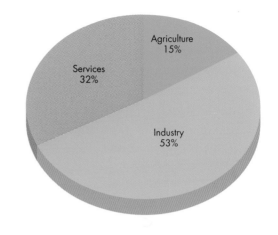

▲ Economy by sector

UNEMPLOYMENT

Until the 1990s, unemployment did not exist in China. But as the country has shifted increasingly to a market economy, many Chinese people have found themselves out of work. In 1999 and 2000, state-owned enterprises (SOEs) were still the greatest providers of jobs in China. As increasing numbers of inefficient SOEs have been closed by the government, many of their former employees have been unable to find alternative work. China's unemployment rate is officially about 3.5 percent, but this figure takes into account only urban unemployment. Millions of "surplus" unskilled, rural laborers are not included in the official unemployment figures.

THE WEALTH GAP

Despite China's impressive economic growth, the vast majority of Chinese people still live in poverty. Most people in rural China have not experienced the benefits of the economic boom, and millions have migrated to the cities and industrialized areas seeking work and better wages. In the years between 1984 and 2004, more than two hundred million people moved to the cities to look for work. By 2024, another

▼ A farmer uses a water buffalo to pull a plow in the province of Guizhou, in southern China.

▶ Chinese shoppers load their purchases into their car after a trip to the IKEA store in Beijing.

three hundred million migrants are expected to join them. The wealth gap between urban and rural China is a direct result of the country's overall economic success. In 2003, the average income for an urban worker in China was U.S.$1,024, while rural workers earned U.S.$317—less than one-third of the amount of money earned by urban workers. The Chinese government recognizes that growing economic inequality is a major challenge for the future, and it has pledged to devote resources to raising farmers' incomes.

WORKERS' RIGHTS

In China, it is illegal for workers to organize independent unions or to strike, and protests against unfair conditions are strongly suppressed by the Communist government. Furthermore, while Chinese labor law provides strong protection for workers' rights, these laws are often poorly enforced. Violations such as forced labor, child labor, excessive overtime, substandard wages, and hazardous working conditions are common. The average income for most Chinese workers remains low, and China still ranks as a poor country by international standards.

? Did You Know?

Each year, eleven out of every one thousand Chinese workers die in industrial accidents.

Focus on: The Pearl River Delta

The Pearl River delta consists of Hong Kong, Macao, and the province of Guangdong. Twenty-five years ago, farmland and small rural villages dominated this area. Today, it is one of the fastest growing regions in China. More than one-half of the world's population is within five hours flying time of Hong Kong, making Hong Kong an attractive economic center. In recent years, many

Hong Kong industries have moved to mainland China, fueling China's massive economic growth. Shenzhen, an area located in Guangdong, was China's first special economic zone. It is now the world's top exporter of watches, telephones, radios, toys, footwear, and clothing, and it is being marketed as China's science and technology city of the future.

CHAPTER 8

Global Connections

Throughout most of the twentieth century, China was isolated from the rest of the world. Other countries saw China as remote and inward-looking. Since the late 1970s, however, reforms introduced by the Communist government have opened up the country to the outside world, particularly in the area of trade, free markets, and foreign investments. Despite its abundance of natural resources, China imports huge amounts of raw materials from other countries to fulfill the needs of its manufacturing industries.

COMPETING WITH THE WORLD

China strengthened its entry into the global market by joining the World Trade Organization (WTO) in 2001. The aim of this organization is to make trade easier between member countries, and entry into the WTO has required China's Communist party government to introduce more reforms, such reducing tariffs on imported goods and allowing more foreign access to its huge internal market.

The main attraction for many foreign companies setting up in China has been the low cost of production, based on low wages and tax breaks given by the Chinese government. Some people have complained that

◀ The China World Trade Center in Beijing opened for business in 1990. It is marketed as "the place where China meets the world."

these incentives give companies in China unfair advantages, because manufacturers in Western countries are unable to compete with China's prices. But businesses around the world are increasingly buying their goods from Chinese suppliers or moving their factory work to China to take advantage of the cheaper costs.

China is now the world's largest consumer of many industrial commodities and raw materials. Its great demand for raw materials has benefited some countries. For example, China's demand for leather for its shoe factories has revived the leather industry in Brazil. China's booming demand for oil, however, was a major reason for the increase in global oil prices in 2004. To ensure access to the resources it needs, China is increasingly investing in other countries. For example, the China National Petroleum Company has invested U.S.$700 million in Kazakhstan to secure future supplies of oil.

GLOBAL RELATIONSHIPS

China recognizes the importance of establishing good relationships with other countries—the United States, in particular—for its future prosperity and security. It is one of only five permanent members of the United Nations Security Council, the branch of the UN that maintains peace and security between nations. Under the Nuclear Nonproliferation Treaty, the five permanent members are the only countries in the world permitted to possess nuclear weapons. Since North Korea admitted in 2002 that it had been developing nuclear weapons, China has supported a nuclear-free Korean peninsula and has played an important diplomatic role mediating between the United States and North Korea.

THE CHINESE ABROAD

China has a long history of trading with other countries. For thousands of years, silk was exported along the "Silk Road," the overland trade route that linked China with countries to the west. Many Chinese merchants moved to Southeast Asia and large Chinese settlements were created in Java, Malaya, Vietnam, Thailand, Singapore, and the Philippines. During the eighteenth and nineteenth centuries, however, China became increasingly isolated from the rest of the world. During the

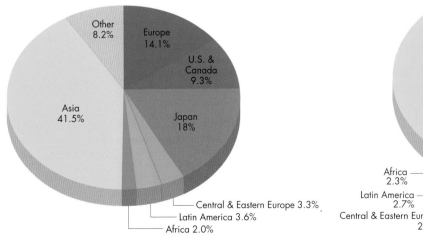

▲ Import origins as percentage of world total

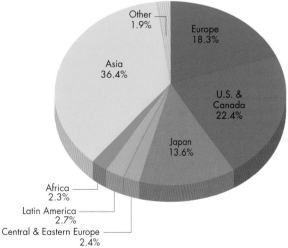

▲ Export destinations as percentage of world total

▲ A wooden bus with open sides like a streetcar takes passengers beneath a Chinese-style bridge in San Francisco's Chinatown. Many major cities around the world have thriving Chinese communities.

nineteenth century and large parts of the twentieth century, China's isolationism was a tactic to prevent the spread of Western influence within its borders. China's government imposed strict controls to prevent people from leaving the country, but in spite of these restrictions, many people escaped, fleeing famine, poverty, or war. By 1854, an estimated twenty-four hundred Chinese were in Australia working in the gold mines. By 1857, the number had risen to over twenty-five thousand. It is also thought that over twenty-five thousand Chinese people took part in the California gold rush in 1852.

Many of these emigrants were unable to return to China and settled overseas. Cities such as San Francisco, New York City, Vancouver, and Toronto, in North America; Sydney, Melbourne, and Brisbane, in Australia; and London, in Britain, all have a Chinatown—an area full of Chinese shops and restaurants. Today there are over 1.5 million Chinese people living in the United States, more than 500,000 in Australia, and about 400,000 in Britain.

HUMAN TRAFFICKING

The desire to move abroad is still strong among many Chinese people, but China's government continues to impose restrictions on leaving the country and on entry to many other countries. As a result, illegal trafficking in human beings has become a problem. People are enticed by stories of better lives abroad to pay high fees to "snakeheads." For around U.S.$12,000—a huge amount of money in China—snakeheads arrange for people to be smuggled out of China, most frequently to Japan or Britain. Wages in Britain, even in illegal employment, are ten times what a Chinese worker could earn at home. Once settled and working, Chinese immigrants often send large amounts of money back to their families in China, making significant contributions to household incomes.

CULTURAL CONTRIBUTIONS

As Chinese people have settled abroad, they have taken their own ways of life with them. Some aspects of Chinese culture have become very well-known all over the globe. Chinese cooking is recognized as one of the great cuisines of the world and has become popular around the world. Martial arts such as tai chi and kung fu have become very popular in the West. Chinese ideas about design and style have also had a major impact, particularly ideas based on the ancient Chinese practice of feng shui. According to feng shui, energy flows through us and around us, and balancing this energy by arranging objects in certain ways is important to a healthy and successful life. Such ideas have become increasingly popular in the West in the last twenty years.

▼ Vancouver, British Columbia, in Canada, has a large Chinese population, and parts of the city cater specifically to this community. This Chinese supermarket is in Vancouver's Chinatown district.

Focus on: The Problem of Human Trafficking

In June 2000, fifty-eight out of a group of sixty Chinese people were discovered dead in an airtight container when a truck that had just crossed the English Channel from Zeebrugge arrived in the British port of Dover. Each of the would-be immigrants had paid U.S.$20,000 to a snakehead to smuggle them into Britain and had traveled for weeks via Yugoslavia, Hungary, Austria, France, and the Netherlands. Before leaving the Netherlands, the driver closed the container's air vent to prevent his cargo from being spotted at immigration checks. When dock workers at Dover searched the container, they found that only two of the group were still alive.

CHAPTER 9

Transportation and Communications

China is struggling to modernize its infrastructure. Its transportation system is under great pressure to cope with its fast-growing economy, its huge population, and the vast distances across the country. As China's people become wealthier, there is an increasing demand for cars as well as a need for more efficient forms of transportation to help open up poorer, inland areas.

▼ Passengers board a domestic flight at Beijing Capital International Airport. Air travel has become increasingly important as China's economy has developed, and China now has the fastest growing air transportation market in the world.

TRANSPORTATION SYSTEMS

Like everything else in China, the transportation networks are growing at a dramatic rate. There is an urgent need to modernize and expand the country's transportation systems to take raw materials to factories and manufactured goods to cities and ports. Rivers and waterways carry about one-third of China's internal freight, while the railroads carry 50 percent. The Chinese rail system is run and largely funded by the government. Development of the rail system is a priority, and future plans include the construction of China's first express passenger service, which will link the cities of Beijing and Tianjin. The line is due

to open in 2008, and other similar lines are planned for the Yangtze delta and the Pearl River delta.

Air travel is important in a country as large as China. The country has international airports in Beijing, Shanghai, and Hong Kong and over three hundred smaller airports with paved runways. Many airports have been rebuilt and enlarged, and small airlines are growing rapidly.

The difference between roads in the urban and rural areas of China is stark. A road network links China's main cities, and five highways now run around the capital, Beijing, to handle the city's traffic congestion. Many rural communities, however, are not served by roads and remain hard to reach.

Transport & Communications Data

- 🗁 Total roads: 1,096,909 miles/1,765,222 km
- 🗁 Total paved roads: 245,708 miles/ 395,410 km
- 🗁 Total unpaved roads: 851,201 miles/ 1,369,812 km
- 🗁 Total railroads: 229,849 miles/70,058 km
- 🗁 Major airports: 383
- 🗁 Cars per 1,000 people: 7
- 🗁 Cellular phones per 1,000 people: 161
- 🗁 Personal computers per 1,000 people: 28
- 🗁 Internet users per 1,000 people: 46

Source: World Bank and CIA World Factbook

▲ Smog envelops the city as vehicles crawl along a major road in Beijing. China's capital is committed to improving its air quality before the 2008 Olympic Games, which it will host.

? Did You Know?

China has built enough roads since 1990 to loop sixteen times around the equator. The total length of these roads is about 400,000 miles (640,000 km).

Focus on: The Railroad to Lhasa

Some areas of China still remain remote and hard to reach. The city of Lhasa, in Tibet, can only be reached by air or by winding mountain roads. The government is now building a 708-mile (1,140 km) railroad to link the city with the rest of China. It will be the highest-altitude railway in the world, and it will cut across vast areas of grassland, lakes, and mountains, causing some concern for the impact the project will have on the environment. While the railroad will bring jobs to this remote area, many Tibetans see it as another way that China is increasing its political control over them. The railroad to Lhasa is due to open in 2007.

PERSONAL TRANSPORTATION

There are 300 million bicycles in China. Bicycles are still the most common form of personal transportation in the country. But the familiar image of China's city streets filled with bicycles is changing. In 1990, the country had only one million cars; by 2003, it had ten times this number. In spite of this rise in car ownership, only 7 out of every 1,000 Chinese people has a car, compared to 1 out of every 1.5 people in the United States.

THE CHINESE MEDIA

The Chinese government is heavily involved in all aspects of the country's media, including newspapers, TV, radio, and the Internet. It places many restrictions on what is written or broadcast. The changes that are taking place as China turns to a more open, market economy, however, are making it increasingly difficult for its government to control the media as tightly as it has in the past.

THE INTERNET IN CHINA

Its approach to the Internet shows the dilemma faced by China's government. While officials want to encourage Chinese people to keep up with and use the latest Internet technology, they also want to control the information available to people in China on the World Wide Web. China now has more than 100 million Internet users, the second largest number in the world after the United States. A large percentage of China's Internet users are located in the major cities and in the coastal commercial centers, while only a tiny proportion of people in the undeveloped rural areas in the western part of the country have access to the Internet.

▼ Chinese officials confiscate computers from an illegal Internet café in Shunde, in southern China, in January 2004. Since 2001, the Chinese government has tightened its control on Internet cafés throughout the country.

Many people in China use Internet cafés to access the World Wide Web, but in recent years, the government has closed down thousands of these cafés because they failed to abide by the strict laws concerning the services they can provide. China's government also blocks access to many foreign Web sites and requires some Internet service providers (ISPs) to record details of the people who use their services. While search engines such as Google do operate in China, information forbidden by the government—including information on Tibet, SARS (severe acute respiratory syndrome), and the banned religious group Falun Gong—is blocked by the government.

In spite of these restrictions, closer contact with the West through travel and business, as well as through the media, is increasingly influencing the opinions of many young and educated people in China. Television satellite dishes are able to pick up programs from Hong Kong and Taiwan, and China now has the biggest market in the world for cellular phones.

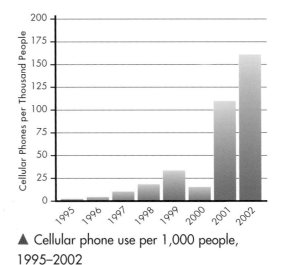

◀ A young rickshaw driver in Beijing sends text messages to his friends on his cellular phone as he waits for his next customer.

Focus on: Text Messaging in China

Text messaging has become very popular in China, particularly because it is impossible to censor. During the SARS epidemic, the government imposed a strict media blackout. Many Chinese people first heard about SARS through their cellular phones. A text message reading, "There is a fatal flu in Guangzhou" was sent over 120 million times in three days. As a direct result of texting, China's government was forced to admit the existence of the virus.

▲ Cellular phone use per 1,000 people, 1995–2002

CHAPTER 10

Education and Health

The Chinese education and health systems are controlled and run by the government. The country's government struggles to educate and provide adequate health facilities for its 1.3 billion people.

▲ A class in a rural school in central China. In addition to Chinese, these children will learn to read and write at least one foreign language, most likely English. In contrast, their parents were lucky if they learned how to read and write in Chinese.

EDUCATION FOR ALL

Providing education for its vast population is a huge challenge for the Chinese government. Nevertheless, much of China's population is well-educated. One-child couples pin a lot of hope on their only child doing well in school, passing exams, and getting a good job, so that he or she can support them later in life. Since 1986, attending school has been compulsory for at least nine years. Children are expected

to work hard, and even primary-school-age children often have several hours of homework every night. Going to school is taken for granted by almost all school-aged children in the country's cities and towns. In poor, rural areas, however, some students struggle to stay in school because they have trouble affording the fees charged at all levels of education in China. Even the official media in China admits that as many as five million children between the ages of seven and eleven do not go to school because their parents cannot afford it.

In many schools, class sizes are large—up to fifty or sixty pupils—and the school day is long—starting at 7 A.M. and finishing after 5 P.M. Students often take additional courses during

Education and Health Data

- 📁 Life expectancy at birth male: 69.0
- 📁 Life expectancy at birth female: 72.4
- 📁 Infant mortality rate per 1,000: 31
- 📁 Under-five mortality rate per 1,000: 39
- 📁 Physicians per 1,000 people: 1.4
- 📁 Health expenditure as % of GDP: 5.5
- 📁 Education expenditure as % of GDP: 2.2
- 📁 Primary school net enrollment %: 93
- 📁 Student-teacher ratio, primary: 19.6
- 📁 Adult literacy % age 15+: 90.9

Source: United Nations Agencies and World Bank

vacations. Partly because of the need to learn large numbers of complex Chinese characters, schools often adopt rote-learning methods, requiring students to memorize their lessons. In 2004, however, the government stated that it wanted education to encourage children to think for themselves more and become what it described as "well-rounded citizens." This change is a direct result of the move toward a more business-oriented society and the need for people who are both creative and flexible.

HIGHER EDUCATION

In a country of 1.3 billion people, China has only 2.5 million university places, and competition for them is intense. China has failed to expand its university and college enrollment because—in spite of the government's stated commitment to education—its public expenditure on education is among the lowest in the world. China is ranked 119th out of 130 countries in terms of the amount it spends per capita on education. It spends half the amount of money spent on education in developed countries.

Loans and scholarships are available to pay for higher education. Although many graduates are assigned jobs, some are now permitted to choose their jobs. Internet-based, distance learning has become increasingly popular since 1998.

▲ Two medical students from Mongolia pose proudly in front of their university motto outside a university building in Xi'an, in central China. They will be among the first doctors from their villages.

Focus on: Shortages in School Funding

In 2001, a massive explosion killed at least thirty-seven children and four teachers in a rural primary school in Fang Lin village, in Jiangxi, one of China's poorest provinces. It was later discovered that the school was using pupils as young as eight years old to assemble fireworks in order to boost its income. Funding shortages have prompted some schools in China to seek additional ways of earning money. Many schools in China, particularly those in rural areas where schools receive less government funding, hire out their students as cheap labor to earn income.

HEALTH CARE

After the founding of the People's Republic of China, a health system was set up to provide basic care that was free and widely available. As a result, life expectancy in China increased from thirty-five years in 1949 to sixty-five years in the mid-1970s. Since the introduction of economic reforms in the late 1970s, however, a big gap has opened up between urban and rural areas in the availability of health care.

The leading causes of death in China are similar to those in the West: cancer and heart disease. Through countrywide campaigns to improve sanitation and hygiene, epidemic diseases such as cholera, scarlet fever, and typhoid fever have almost been eradicated. Tuberculosis (TB), a disease that is now virtually unknown in developed countries, still causes thousands of deaths every year in China, mainly in rural areas.

DIFFERENCES IN CARE

Life expectancy in China is now 69 years for men and 72.4 years for women. These statistics conceal the huge differences between health care in urban and rural areas in China. The move toward a market economy during the 1980s caused the old systems for funding health care to break down. As clinics and hospitals ran out of money, they began to charge patients for treatment and medicines. For the majority of people in the wealthier urban areas, these costs could be covered by health insurance. In the poor, rural areas, however, few people have health insurance, and millions of people cannot afford even the most basic medical attention. The whole system is under strain, and in an emergency, such as the outbreak of SARS in 2002, it struggles to cope with the problem.

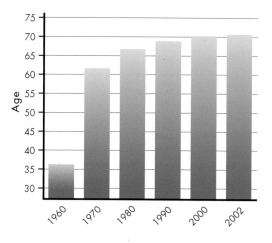

▲ Life expectancy at birth 1960-2002

SARS

An outbreak of severe acute respiratory syndrome (SARS) started in Guangdong Province in southern China in November 2002. It quickly spread to Hong Kong and to other parts of mainland China, including Beijing. In April 2003, the Chinese government was forced to apologize for its slow response to the disease, which spread all around the world. The threat of SARS caused the city authorities in Beijing to close down schools, theaters, movie theaters, and bars to try to contain the disease. SARS killed 349 people in China in 2003.

TRADITIONAL MEDICINE

Although many Chinese medical professionals practice Western medicine, many people in China still use traditional Chinese medicine. Sometimes doctors use a combination of

? Did You Know?

The Chinese smoke 30 percent of the world's cigarettes. It is estimated that 200 million Chinese men smoke and that half of this number could die from tobacco-related diseases before 2030.

Western and traditional Chinese treatments. The theory behind traditional Chinese medicine is that dynamic energy, known as *qi*, runs in channels, called meridians, through the body. Illness occurs when the meridians become blocked. Chinese medicine aims to maintain or restore harmony in the body using acupuncture, herbal medicine, and massage. Traditional Chinese medicine uses thousands of plant species as well as animal parts in its treatments. China has about 250,000 doctors trained in traditional medicine, although there are also thousands of unofficial practitioners.

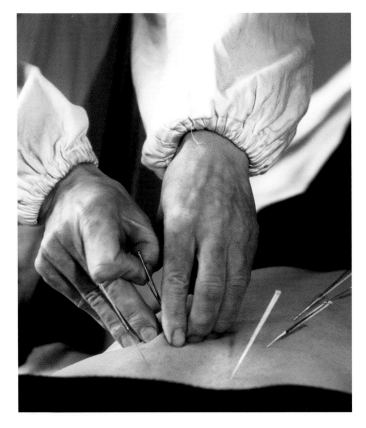

▶ A patient receives acupuncture in a hospital in Chengdu, in the province of Sichuan. Acupuncture involves piercing certain points of the body with thin needles.

Focus on: HIV/AIDS in China

According to the United Nations, ten million people in China could be living with HIV/AIDS by 2010. Although this figure is small as a proportion of the country's total population, many believe that China has the world's fastest growing rate of HIV infection. Many people have caught the virus through intravenous drug use or prostitution. In some rural areas, poor workers have contracted the virus from selling their blood to illegal blood banks that used unsterilized equipment. The Chinese government denied that there was a problem until 2001, when it finally

admitted that the country was facing a serious crisis. Since then, the Chinese media has been encouraged to spread "correct information" about HIV/AIDS in an attempt to prevent further spread of the disease.

▶ Commuters in Nanyang, Henan Province, look at advertisements on the grab-handles in a bus. The crossed red ribbon is an international symbol for AIDS awareness.

CHAPTER 11

Culture and Religion

During the Cultural Revolution, Mao Zedong exhorted the Chinese to turn their backs on the "four olds"—old ideas, old culture, old customs, and old habits. Today, China's rich cultural heritage is once again acknowledged and celebrated.

THE FAMILY

The idea of the family is very important in China. Several generations of one family often live together, and the elderly are respected and cared for by their relatives. These traditional values, however, are changing. Divorce is increasing, and 14 percent of households now consist of either a childless single adult or a childless couple who both work.

▼ A family reunion in the province of Henan in 2002. The family sits around a table together to eat a traditional meal. The food is placed on a revolving platform at the center of the table so that each person may help themselves to a little of each dish.

FOOD

Chinese food varies considerably from region to region. In the north of the country, where wheat is the staple crop, meals are based on noodles. In the south, rice is the staple food. Rice is eaten so regularly in the southern regions that a common greeting is, "Have you eaten rice yet?" There are four main styles of regional cuisine. Cantonese cooking (from Guangdong) uses stir-frying and steaming as the main methods of cooking fresh ingredients. In the cold north, wheat noodles, dumplings, and steamed breads are the basic foods. Peking (Beijing) duck and Mongolian hot-pot are popular dishes. Food from Sichuan, China's largest province, is characterized by spices and chili peppers; one popular dish is hot-and-sour

▲ Street vendors prepare food in Urumqi, in the province of Xinjiang, in northwestern China. The food is cooked and kept hot over a brazier.

soup. The cuisine of eastern China is based on rice, and sugar is used to sweeten many of its rich dishes. All over China, people eat from bowls and with chopsticks. Stalls selling snacks such as kebabs, noodles, or dumplings are found on the streets of the larger cities.

? Did You Know?

China's three most popular surnames—Li, Wang, and Zhang—belong to about 270 million Chinese people, a number almost equal to the entire population of the United States.

RELIGION AND COMMUNISM

Throughout China's history, the three main religions in the country have been Taoism, Confucianism, and Buddhism. After 1949, the Communists discouraged the practice of any religion, closed down monasteries, and converted many temples for other uses. During the Cultural Revolution, religion was attacked as part of China's "old" culture. This situation eased when the reformers came to power in 1978, but the Communist government still does not encourage religion and, officially, China is an atheist country. In order to improve relations with some of its minority groups and as a result of pressure from outside China, however, the government now allows more freedom for people to practice religion.

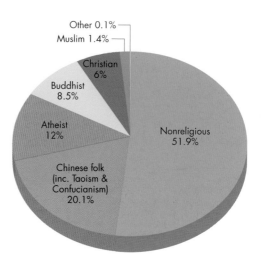

▲ China's major religions

RELIGIONS IN CHINA

Taoism is a native Chinese religion and its founder, Laozi, is said to have lived during the sixth century B.C. One of its fundamental teachings is that people are part of the wider environment and that there is no such thing as self. The teachings of Confucius emphasize the importance of the family and order in society. Buddhism came to China from India as early as the first century A.D. It is estimated that as many as one hundred million Chinese follow the Buddhist religion. Despite having been suppressed for years, these belief systems continue to have a major influence on the way Chinese people behave and think.

Western missionaries brought Christianity to China in the seventeenth century, although it is possible that Christians visited China as early as the fifth century. The number of Christians in China today is estimated at seventy-nine million. Contacts between the Islamic world and China started in the seventh century. The T'ang emperor Yung-Wei approved the establishment of the first Chinese mosque at Ch'ang-an (Xi'an)—a building that still stands today. Unofficial estimates put the

▲ A Buddhist pilgrim spins prayer wheels mounted along a wall of the Potala Palace in Lhasa, Tibet. Buddhists believe that spinning these wheels releases their prayers.

Muslim population in China today at around eighteen million. The main Muslim groups in the country are the Hui and the Uyghurs.

FESTIVALS

Festivals are a major part of Chinese life. The Chinese New Year is a big event, and it is celebrated with dragon dances, lion dances, and firecrackers. Another important festival is Ching Ming, or Remembrance of Ancestors Day. On this day, people visit their family tombs to clean them and to leave food and offerings for the spirits of their ancestors.

The lion dance is performed at most Chinese festivals, particularly at Chinese New Year festivals and at weddings. The dance is performed by two people, with one controlling the highly decorated lion's head while the other moves the body and tail of the lion under a cloth attached to the head. The dance is believed to bring both happiness and good luck.

The Taoist Bun Festival is unique to Cheung Chau, a small island in Hong Kong. For this festival, huge structures of bamboo are covered with bread buns. In the past, young people scrambled up the towers to grab as many buns as they could. Since 1978, when several injuries occurred, the buns have been handed out.

Kites are also an important part of Chinese culture. They have religious significance because they are seen as a means of making contact with the gods in heaven. It takes many years to become a master kite-maker, although most Chinese boys and girls learn to make their own kites at an early age. Weifang, in the province of Shandong, is famous for its kite-making and kite-flying customs. Every April, people from all over the world come to the annual kite festival in Weifang.

▼ Chinese dancers perform the lion dance in a park in Beijing in February 2005. This ceremony marked the beginning of the Chinese New Year celebrations.

CHAPTER 12

Leisure and Tourism

Until the 1980s, weekends were unknown to most Chinese people. For most people in China, leisure time was restricted by the amount of work they had to do and the money they needed to earn. Working seven days a week in a factory or on a farm was common.

LEISURE TIME

The government introduced two-day weekends during the 1990s, and most people now work only five days a week. Since 1999, the country has also had three week-long holidays, known as Golden Weeks, that are based around the Chinese New Year, in late January or early February; May Day; and National Day, in October. These holidays have boosted the economy, because millions of Chinese spend money traveling to see relatives, shopping,

and celebrating. Many people, however, dislike these set holidays because tourist destinations are crowded and prices are often inflated. It is possible that the Golden Weeks will be replaced with a more flexible system of holidays.

Older people in China, especially men, can be seen playing games in street-side cafes and bars all over the country. In particular, the clicking of tiles resounds through streets and alleyways as people play the popular game mah jongg. Other popular games are chess and cards.

▼ Tai chi is popular throughout China, especially among the elderly. These people are practicing tai chi early in the morning in a park in Shanghai. Tai chi involves the coordination of mind, body, and breathing in a series of slow, controlled movements.

SPORTS

Martial arts (or *wushu*) were developed in China nearly three thousand years ago as a form of self-defense and survival. They aim to improve physical ability, overall health, and willpower and are now considered to be as much a sport as a way of fighting. Chinese martial arts include karate, tai chi, and kung fu. It is often possible to see people practicing tai chi in public parks early in the morning. Tai chi has been claimed to reduce stress levels and lower blood pressure.

Chinese people enjoy watching and playing many sports. Many of them excel at sports such as table tennis, badminton, basketball, and golf. In addition, they are passionate about soccer, and the country's national team reached the World Cup finals for the first time in 2002. Chinese athletes won thirty-two gold medals in the 2004 Olympic Games in Athens. China won gold medals in weightlifting, tae kwon do, table tennis, badminton, diving, shooting, swimming, canoeing, gymnastics, wrestling, volleyball, and judo. China was second only to the United States in the total number of medals won.

? Did You Know?

The Chinese basketball player Wang Zhizhi was the first Asian person to play in the National Basketball Association (NBA). He was signed by the Dallas Mavericks in 2001. Other Chinese players who have played in the NBA are Yao Ming and Mengke Bateer.

▼ China's goalkeeper, Liu Yunfei, saves a goal during the Asian Cup soccer final against Japan in Beijing, in August 2004. Japan eventually won 3–1.

TOURISM

Tourism is yet another growth industry in China, with the number of foreign visitors rocketing from 710,000 in 1978 to 36.8 million in 2003. Most of these visitors come from China's near neighbors in Asia, such as Japan and Korea, and from Russia. Over 800,000 people from the United States and nearly 300,000 from Britain came to China in 2003. Many visitors to China are Chinese people who live in other countries or business travelers, but an increasing number of tourists on luxury tours and as independent backpackers also visit China. It is estimated that China will be the world's top tourist destination by 2020, with up to 130 million visitors a year.

In the past, China's government did little to encourage visitors. Now, however, it recognizes that tourism is yet another way in which it can make money. Most of China, including Tibet, is

Tourism in China

- 🗁 Tourist arrivals, millions: 36.8
- 🗁 Earnings from tourism in U.S.$: 20,385,000,000
- 🗁 Tourism as % of foreign earnings: 6
- 🗁 Tourist departures, millions: 16.6
- 🗁 Expenditure on tourism in U.S.$: 15,398,000,000

Source: World Bank

▲ The famous Terracotta Army near Xi'an, in central China, was discovered in 1974. It consists of more than six thousand clay figures of people and horses in three burial pits that date back to the Qin dynasty (221–206 B.C.). Today, the Terracotta Army is one of China's main tourist attractions.

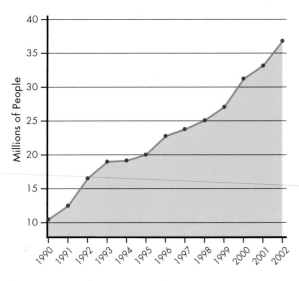

▲ International tourist arrivals, 1990–2002

open to foreign tourists, although access to some western areas is still restricted. The country has many historic and cultural attractions, including the Great Wall of China; the Forbidden City, in Beijing; and the Terracotta Army, near Xi'an. The country is now developing new attractions to pull in more tourists, particularly in the field of sports. In 2004, a huge, new, world-championship racing track was opened as part of the Formula One circuit. In addition, and with much controversy because of its human rights record, Beijing is scheduled to host the 2008 Olympic Games.

The phenomenal growth of cities such as Shanghai has become a tourist attraction in itself. Some people take boat trips to view Shanghai's ultramodern skyline that includes the futuristic Oriental Pearl TV Tower—one of the tallest buildings in the world. In contrast, other tourists are attracted to China by the remoteness of some of the areas in the west, such as Tibet.

Although overseas travel for Chinese people is still restricted by the government, some of these restrictions are being lifted. In 1993, just under 4 million Chinese people traveled abroad. By 2002, this number was 16.6 million. In 2004, an agreement was reached between China and the European Union that makes it easier for Chinese citizens to apply for tourist visas to twenty-nine European nations that have been granted "approved destination status" by China.

Focus on: The 2008 Beijing Olympics

The decision to award the 2008 Olympic Games to Beijing was highly controversial. Human rights organizations such as Human Rights Watch and Amnesty International have expressed concerns that, by granting the Olympic Games to Beijing, the world is condoning China's human rights record. Some Chinese dissidents claim that China is using the Olympic Games to present itself as a global power with an acceptable human rights record. Human-rights organizations also wonder what will happen when thousands of international athletes and journalists arrive in a country that suppresses and controls the media. On the other hand, it is possible that, as China comes under the spotlight of the world, the event will act as an impetus for the government to demonstrate that it is changing and that China is coming into line with international laws having to do with human rights.

▶ This clock in Tiananmen Square, in Beijing, is counting down to the 2008 Olympic Games.

CHAPTER 13

Environment and Conservation

China's environment is paying the price for the country's rapid economic development. Several factors are having a major effect on the country's environment, including the pressures of supporting such a large population with the produce from its relatively small area of land that is suitable for cultivation and the extremely rapid rate of industrialization.

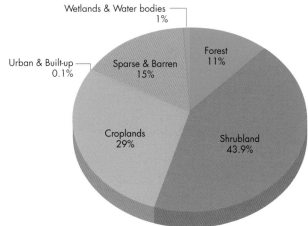

Wetlands & Water bodies 1%

Forest 11%

Urban & Built-up 0.1%

Sparse & Barren 15%

Croplands 29%

Shrubland 43.9%

▲ Habitat type as percentage of total area

WILDLIFE UNDER THREAT

The diversity of wildlife in China is among the greatest in the world, with a huge variety of animal species. Many animals in China, however, are on the endangered species list, including the snow leopard, tiger, ibis, elephant, and, most famously, the giant panda. These animals are threatened with extinction by a combination of loss of habitat to human development, illegal hunting, and natural disasters such as floods.

DAMS

Many animal conservationists are worried about the number of hydroelectric power projects being planned in China. The construction of a

▲ This picture of a snow leopard was taken on a wildlife reserve in northern China. It is estimated that there are around two thousand snow leopards in China, but they are seriously threatened by poaching, habitat loss, and shortage of prey.

? Did You Know?

By 2010, China plans to have eighteen hundred nature reserves. These reserves will cover about 16.14 percent of the country's territory.

dam seriously decreases the flow of water downstream from the dam and has a major impact on river habitats. Conservationists are particularly concerned about the *baiji*, a type of freshwater dolphin that lives in the Yangtze River. It was estimated in 2003 that there were fewer than one hundred baiji left in the river.

The construction of the Three Gorges Dam has significantly changed the baiji's habitat, and the baiji is expected to become extinct in the near future. In 2004, plans for a huge dam system on the Nu River in southern China were shelved for environmental reasons, but many other dams are planned elsewhere.

Environmental and Conservation Data

🗀 Forested area as % of total land area: 11

🗀 Protected area as % of total land area: 7.8

🗀 Number of protected areas: 822

SPECIES DIVERSITY

Category	Known species (1992–2002)	Threatened species (2002)
Mammals	394	79
Breeding birds	618	74
Reptiles	424	31
Amphibians	340	1
Fish	395	32
Plants	32,200	168

Source: World Resources Institute

Focus on: The Giant Panda

The giant panda is one of the best-known symbols of China. It is found only in southwest China and lives exclusively on a diet of bamboo shoots. It is one of the world's most endangered species, facing threats both from the loss of its habitat and from poaching. The Chinese government has set up more than thirty reserves to protect the giant panda, and near Chengdu, in the province of Sichuan, a breeding center has been created. Some of the pandas at this center are raised in such a way that they can be reintroduced to the wild. It is estimated that there are only about sixteen hundred giant pandas remaining alive.

▶ A giant panda in Chengdu eats bamboo shoots.

▲ A girl in the center of Conjiang, located in the province of Guizhou, covers her nose and mouth to keep out dust.

DEFORESTATION

Over the last fifty years, vast areas of China's forests have been cut down for construction purposes and for fuel. This deforestation has caused soil erosion, particularly in areas of high rainfall, and has had a devastating impact on river catchments, increasing the incidence of flooding in some of China's major river regions. In 1998, devastating floods along the Yangtze that killed four thousand people were partly blamed on excessive deforestation along the upper reaches of the Yangtze and other rivers. As a result, China completely banned logging. To meet the demand for timber, the country increased its imports. The increase in the amount of timber exported to China from Russia and Southeast Asia, however, has put great pressure on forests in these regions.

DESERTIFICATION

Desertification is a major problem in China, affecting nearly a quarter of the country's total land area. The biggest problems are in the northwest, where deserts are growing at an alarming rate. One reason for the increase in desertification lies in the rapid expansion of cities in eastern China, which reduces the amount of farmland available and leads to the opening up of new areas in the northwest to agriculture. Land has been cleared of trees and plowed up for planting crops, exposing the thin soil to erosion from wind and rain. In other places, overgrazing of animals has stripped the land of its vegetation. In the Takla Makan Desert, sand frequently buries houses and crops. In addition, the effects of desertification are felt far beyond the deserts of the northwest. Sandstorms often darken the skies over China's eastern cities, far away from the deserts. Measures to fight desertification include projects to plant trees. However, the prospect of a Chinese dust bowl and its impacts on food production present serious challenges to China's ability to produce the large amounts of food it needs to feed its vast population.

POLLUTION

China has developed its industries with little thought for the environment. The country's high consumption of coal has made it the world's second largest source of CO_2 after the United States. Many Chinese cities are often shrouded in a thick smog of pollution, with unhealthy levels of toxic particles in the air. In addition, many rivers in China are polluted with chemicals, untreated waste from factories, and untreated sewage.

China is now engaged in a massive effort to clean up its own environment and, consequently, the environment of the world.

Since 1966, China has shut down sixty thousand inefficient industrial boilers, and hundreds of small power stations have also been closed. In 1993, China's government introduced laws abolishing ozone-depleting substances. Since then, it has funded the exploration of more environmentally friendly technologies and energy sources, such as wind power and solar energy.

? Did You Know?

According to the World Health Organization, some of the world's most polluted cities are in China. These cities include Linfen, Yangquan, and Datong—all in the coal-producing province of Shanxi. Beijing, which is working to improve its air quality before the 2008 Olympics, was twenty-eighth on the WHO list.

▼ Factories in an industrial complex on the outskirts of Beijing belch out smoke and fumes.

CHAPTER 14

Future Challenges

China's headlong dash for growth has raised concerns about its environment, the size of its population, the often appalling working conditions in the country, and the increasing gap between the country's rich and poor.

PUBLIC WELFARE

Supporting such a huge population places a burden on the state to provide education and health care, both of which are vital to ensure the country's economic development. Like many other countries, China needs to face up to the challenge of the spread of HIV/AIDS. Eventually, China will have to pay the costs of its One-Child Policy. Beginning in about 2020, there will be a reduction in the size of the labor force, and the population will begin to age. In order to enable the country's economy to keep growing and transforming China at a rapid rate, pressure to relax the One-Child Policy is likely to intensify. The imbalance between young men and women also poses a major threat to the healthy, harmonious, and sustainable growth of the nation's population.

▼ The stunning interior of Pudong International Airport in Shanghai, which opened in 1999. Shanghai now has two international airports, reflecting its status as one of the main hubs of China's economic development.

Making women more equal to men in terms of pay and, therefore, in their ability to support their families, may prevent families from wanting only male babies.

ECONOMIC CHANGES

The sustainability of China's economic boom is in question. Some experts think that economic growth has been too fast and unplanned. The changes in the economy have failed to benefit the majority of the Chinese population, and the people who are employed in factories fueling China's economic growth often work in sweatshop conditions. The initial advantages China has had will not last if employment costs rise. If labor costs rise, foreign investors may choose to relocate to countries in which these costs are lower, such as India.

In response to some of these problems, China's government is considering measures to control the pace of economic growth through restraints on investment and lending. By slowing the pace of growth, the government would hope to curb inflation that, if left uncontrolled, would drive up labor costs and reduce China's global competitiveness. Evidence already shows that China's booming economy and incredible demand for commodities— in 2003, China's construction industry consumed 40 percent of the world's cement output— is driving up world prices. Preventing the country's economy from "overheating" is a key challenge for China's government.

CHINA'S UNIQUE CULTURE

More links with other countries through economic development and the growth of the tourist industry mean that China is increasingly coming into contact with Western ideas. Many people welcome these new influences, but others worry that traditional Chinese culture may suffer. China has a difficult balancing act to perform in the future as it struggles to preserve its unique culture while at the same time emerging as a new world superpower.

? Did You Know?

In October 2003, China sent its first astronaut, Yang Liwei, into space. The flight made China only the third country in the world to launch a manned spacecraft into orbit. (The first two were the United States and the Soviet Union.) This event was seen both as a symbol of the great progress China has made and as a symbol of its ambitions for the future.

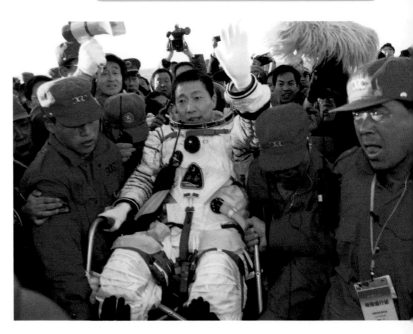

▲ China's first astronaut, Yang Liwei, waves to a large crowd after his safe return to Earth on October 16, 2003.

Time Line

c.1700–c.1027 B.C. Shang dynasty.

771–481 B.C. Chou dynasty.

c.551–c.479 B.C. Life of philosopher Confucius.

453–221 B.C. Warring States period.

221–206 B.C. China is unified under the Qin.

206 B.C.–A.D. 220 Flourishing of intellectual and artistic life under the Han dynasty.

220–588 Wei, Shu, and Wu dynasties: a period of chaos and decline as China is divided into three kingdoms.

581–618 Reunification and centralization of government under the Sui dynasty.

618–907 High point in Chinese civilization under the T'ang dynasty.

907–960 China breaks up into separate states.

960–1279 Reunification of China under the Sung dynasty.

1215 Genghis Khan captures Beijing.

1271–1295 Marco Polo's journey to China.

1279–1368 Mongol Yuan dynasty.

1368–1644 Ming dynasty.

1644–1911 Ch'ing or Manchu dynasty.

1839–1842 First Opium War leads to ceding of Hong Kong and opening of ports to trade.

1858–1860 Second Opium War.

1894–1895 War with Japan.

1911 Last emperor is deposed.

1912 Sun Yat-Sen declares China a republic.

1919 Fourth of May movement in Beijing.

1921 Chinese Communist party founded.

1931 Japan invades Manchuria.

1934–1935 Mao Zedong leads the Long March.

1937–1945 Sino-Japanese War.

1949 Chinese Communists defeat the Nationalists, and Mao Zedong proclaims the People's Republic of China.

1958 The Great Leap Forward begins.

1966 Mao Zedong launches the Great Proletarian Cultural Revolution.

1972 U.S. president Richard Nixon visits China.

1976 Death of Mao Zedong.

1978 Start of economic modernization led by Deng Xiaoping.

1979 Start of One-Child Policy.

1989 Government troops put down Tiananmen Square demonstration.

1993 Work starts on Three Gorges Dam on the Yangtze River.

1997 Hong Kong reverts to China.

1999 Chinese government bans Falun Gong movement.

2001 China joins the World Trade Organization.

2002 Work starts on the South-to-North Water Transfer Project.

2002–2003 Global outbreak of SARS begins in China.

2003 China sends its first astronaut, Yang Liwei, into space.

2005 China announces new policies that make the exchange rate of its currency flexible.

Glossary

acupuncture a centuries-old method of maintaining and restoring harmony in the body by piercing certain points with thin needles

alluvial describes clay and silt that are carried by fast-moving streams and rivers and then deposited when the waters slow down, producing fertile soil

atheist a person who believes no deity exists

autonomous self-governing. In China, the five autonomous regions (*zizhiqu*) have some self-government but remain under the control of the central Communist government

bourgeois a member of the middle, or in Communist countries, capitalist class

cede to surrender or give up

collective farms in Communist countries, groups of farms owned by the state and run by the community

communism a political system that abolishes private ownership and emphasizes common ownership of property and the means of production

democracy a political system in which representatives are chosen by the people in free elections

desertification the process by which fertile land is degraded into barren desert

dissident someone who disagrees with the policies of the government

dust bowl an arid region in which wind erosion causes dust storms

dynasty a series of rulers from the same family who succeed one another in power

elitist a person who believes a particular group of people is superior to other groups

ethnic classified according to membership in racial, cultural, linguistic, or relgious group

floodplain an area of open land through which a river flows and which is sometimes covered by its flood waters

free market an economic system controlled by supply and demand more than by regulations

freight commercial goods carried by trucks, ships, trains, and airplanes

gross domestic product (GDP) the total value of the goods and services produced in a country in a given year

gross national income (GNI) a country's gross domestic product plus the net income it earns from investments in other countries in a given year; also called gross national product (GNP)

guerrilla using tactics of irregular armed forces

hydroelectric power electricity generated from the power of moving bodies of water

industrialization the process of developing factories and manufacturing on a large scale

inflation the increase the general level of prices in a country for goods and services

infrastructure the basic facilities and equipment needed for a country to function

martial arts various styles of armed and unarmed combat developed in the East and usually practiced today as a sport

nationalism a strong commitment to the independence, culture, and interests of one's own country

nomadic moving from place to place rather than living in a settlement

opium a drug produced from the juice of the opium poppy which can be addictive if misused

plateau an area of high, level land

species a group of plants or animals that share common features

tariff a tax on imports

topography the shape of the surface feaures of the Earth

totalitarian describes a form of government that is highly centralized, which controls all aspects of life in a country, and which suppresses opposition

typhoon a violent, rotating storm in the West Pacific or Indian Oceans, also called a cyclone

urbanization movement of people to cities.

Further Information

BOOKS TO READ

Ancient China (Eyewitness Books series)
Arthur Cotterell
(DK Publishing)

China (Countries of the World series)
Carole Goddard
(Facts on File)

Emperor's Silent Army: Terracotta Warriors
of Ancient China
Jane O'Connor
(Viking)

The Forbidden City (Places in History series)
Susie Hodge
(World Almanac Library)

Han Dynasty (Lost Civilizations series)
Myra Immell
(Lucent Books)

Hong Kong (Great Cities of the World series)
Nicola Barber
(World Almanac Library)

Mao Zedong (Judge for Yourself series)
Christine Hatt
(World Almanac Library)

Red Scarf Girl: A Memoir of the Cultural Revolution
Ji-li Jiang
(HarperCollins Children's Books)

Tales from China (Oxford Myths and Legends series)
Retold by Cyril Birch
(Oxford University Press)

USEFUL WEB SITES

Beijing 2008
www.beijing-2008.org

The Economist
www.economist.com/countries/China

Great Wall Across the Yangtze
www.pbs.org/itvs/greatwall/

Secrets of Lost Empires: China Bridge
www.pbs.org/wgbh/nova/lostempires/china/

Visions of China
www.cnn.com/SPECIALS/1999/china.50/

World Almanac for Kids Online: China
www.worldalmanacforkids.com/explore/
nations/china.html

Index

Page numbers in **bold** indicate pictures.

acupuncture 45, **45**
air pollution 39
air transportation 38, **38**, 39
airports 39, 58

baiji 55
basketball 51
Beijing 9, 11, 12, 16, 17, **22**, 29, 33, 38, 39, **39**, 41, 44, 49, 53, **53**, 57, **57**
bicycles 40
Boxer uprising 11
Buddhism 9, 23, 48, **48**

cars 31-32, **31**, 38, 39, 40
cellular phones 31, 39, 41
Chiang Kai-shek 11, 12
Ch'ing dynasty 9, 11, 24, 25
Chinatown 36, **36**, **37**
Chou dynasty 8, 9
Christianity 10, 48
climate 16-17, 54
coal 26, **26**, 27, 28
Communist party 11, 12–13, 22
Confucius/Confucianism 9, **9**, 48
Cultural Revolution 13, 48

Dalai Lama 23, 24, **24**
dams 27–28, **27**, 29, 54–55
danwei (work units) 22
deforestation 56
Deng Xiaoping 13, 30
desertification 56–57
dissidents 22, 53

economy 5, 30–33
  future 59
  "open" zones 31
  Open-Door policy 20
  reforms 13, 30–31, 34
  special economic zones (SEZs) 30, 33
  wealth gap 32–33
education 42–43, **42**, **43**, 58
endangered species 54
energy 26–28
environment 54–57
ethnic groups 18
Everest, Mount 6, 15
exports 6, 31, 33

Falun Gong 23, **23**, 41
family life 46, **46**
farming **4**, 5, 14, 15, 19, 28, **32**, 33
feng shui 37
festivals 49, **49**
feudal system 8, 9
fishing 29, **29**
flag 6
food 37, **46**, 47, **47**

gas 26
geography 6, **7**, 14-15
giant panda 54, 55, **55**
Golden Weeks 50
government 19, 22–23, **22**, 24, 25, 30, 31, 34, 40, 41, 43, 52, 59
Great Leap Forward 13
Great Wall 8, **8**, 9, 53

Hakka 18, **18**
Han Chinese 18, 24

Han dynasty 8, 9
health care 42, 44–45, 58
Himalayas 14, 15
HIV/AIDS 45, **45**, 58
holidays 50
Hong Kong 11, 23, **23**, 24–25, **25**, 33, 39, 41, 44, 49
Huang He 15, 24, 28
Hui 18, 49
human rights 22, 23, 53
human trafficking 36, 37
hydroelectric power (HEP) 26–28

Imperial Palace, Beijing **10**, **12**, **16**
industrialization 12
Internet 22, 39, 40–41
Islam 48–49
isolationism 10-11, 34, 35, 36

Japan 9, 11, 12, 31, 36

kites 49
Korea, North 35

life expectancy 42, 44
lion dance 49, **49**
Long March, the 12

Macao 25, 33
mah-jongg 50
Mao Zedong 12, **12**, 13, **13**, 30
martial arts 37, 51
medicine
  Chinese 44–45
  Western 44–45
migrant workers 21, 33

mineral reserves 26, 29
Mongols 8, 18

Nationalist party (Kuomintang)
    11, 12, 25
nature reserves 54
Nixon, Richard 13
nuclear power 28

oil/petroleum 26, 27, 28, 35
Olympic Games 51, 53, **53**, 57
One-Child Policy 19, **19**, 58–59
opium 10-11
Opium Wars 11, 24
overseas settlement 36, 37

People's Republic of China
    12–13, 18, 25, 44
pollution 57
Polo, Marco 10
population 4, 6, 18–21
    density 20
    growth 18, 19, 20

Qin dynasty 4, 8, 9, 52

railroads 38–39
Red Guards 13, **13**
rivers 14-15, **15**, 26–27, **27**,
    28–29, **29**, 38, 55, 57
sandstorms 17, 56–57

schools 42–43
severe acute respiratory
    syndrome (SARS) 41, 44
Shanghai **5**, **17**, 21, **21**, 31,
    39, 53
Shenzhen 30, 33
Silk Road 9, 35
snow leopard 54, **54**
soccer 51, **51**
South-to-North Water
    Transfer Project 29
Soviet Union 12, 30
space flight 59
Special Administrative Region
    (SAR) 24–25, 33
Sun Yat-sen 11

tai chi 37, **50**, 51
Taiwan 12, 25, 41
Takla Makan Desert **14**, 56
T'ang dynasty 9, 10, 24
Taoism 9, 48, 49
Terracotta Army 52, **52**, 53
Three Gorges Dam 27–28,
    27, 55
Tiananmen Square, Beijing 11,
    12, 22, **53**
Tibet 24, 39, 41, 52
Tibetan plateau 14, 15, 17
time zones 16
tourism 52–53

transportation 6, 38–40
typhoons 17

unemployment 32
United Nations 35
United States 10, 13, 14, 25, 35,
    36, 51, 52
universities 43
urbanization 20–21
Uyghurs 18, 49

water supplies 28–29
Wen Jiabao 13
wildlife 54–55
working conditions 33
World Trade Organization 34

Yang Liwei 59, **59**
Yangtze River 14, 15, **15**, 21, 27,
    27, 28–29, 39, 55, 56
Yuan dynasty 9, 24

Zhongguo 4
Zhuang 18